W9-ATH-454

LIBRARY
UNIV. OF CONNECTICUT
AT AVERY PT.
GROTON, CONN. 06340.

# MAKING WAVES IN FOGGY BOTTOM

*How a new and more scientific approach changed the management system at the State Department.*

Also by ALFRED J. MARROW

NTL institute                    Washington, D.C.

1974

# MAKING WAVES IN FOGGY BOTTOM

*How a new and more scientific approach changed the management system at the State Department.*

By ALFRED J. MARROW, Ph.D.

Copyright © 1974 by Alfred J. Marrow. All rights reserved. No part of this book may be reproduced in any form or by any means, except for the inclusion of brief quotations in a review, without permission in writing. Printed by Pelzer & Green, New York City.

## TO ELLIOT L. RICHARDSON

*who, in his brief stay as
Undersecretary of State,
left a significant imprint
on the management system
of the State Department.*

# *Acknowledgments*

To make an adequate statement of my indebtedness to the many persons who participated in this project is beyond my power. However, some particular words of appreciation are in order.

I must gratefully acknowledge the help of Donald P. Warwick, Marvin Meade, and Theodore Reed, who provided the data assembled by them under the contract with the Institute for Social Research of the University of Michigan.

I have had inestimable help from the observations and judgments of my long-time friends, Chris Argyris and Harry Levinson, who, in numerous ways, influenced the direction of this project.

To my many friends inside and outside the State Department and to my colleagues at National Training Laboratories, I wish to express my lasting appreciation for their invaluable assistance. This project would never have come into being without the innovativeness of William J. Crockett, and the subsequent support of William B. Macomber, and I owe them a great debt of gratitude.

I am equally grateful to The James Marshall Fund, which

has financially supported the preparation and publication of this volume.

Finally, I owe much to Philip Freund and Bernard Collier for their editorial assistance; and to Bea Pelzer for her cheerful patience in handling the many difficult administrative situations that arose during the writing of this book.

THE SECRETARY OF STATE

WASHINGTON

April 12, 1966

Dear Dr. Marrow:

I want to express my personal appreciation for your willingness to assist the Department of State in the performance of its complex assignments.

The contribution which you and the other American business and professional leaders have volunteered is of great significance and represents the highest type of service to one's country.

I look forward to your continued close association with us as we try to fulfill our responsibilities.

Sincerely yours,

Dean Rusk

Dean Rusk

# Foreword

## By Hubert H. Humphrey

Early in my term as Vice President I observed and experienced how complex the American diplomat's job had become in the last two decades. Not only were world diplomatic problems more intense, the pace faster and the potential costs of failure shockingly greater, but many new government agencies were now involved in foreign affairs.

Nevertheless, we still expected the State Department to lead and coordinate. As a United States Senator, I had dealt personally with members of the Department on many matters. Despite my own respect for most of its officers, I agreed with the majority of the Congress and other government leaders who considered the Department rigid, indecisive, and afflicted with dry rot.

In my judgment, the State Department has always had access to plentiful talent. That 10,000 applicants compete in the annual entrance examinations for the Foreign Service and only 150 receive appointments is one indication the level of competence should be high.

The difficulties the Department experienced were significantly due, not to a lack of knowledge and skills on the part of the officers of the Foreign Service, but to faulty administration that prevented the staff's leadership potential from being fully utilized.

The many previous efforts to reorganize the Department had accomplished little. The long needed reforms were invariably blocked.

Therefore, I was pleased to learn in 1965 that Deputy Undersecretary for Administration William Crockett had initiated a major reform program. He had enlisted my longtime friend, Alfred J. Marrow, and a number of other outstanding leaders from the business and professional worlds, to implement far-reaching changes in the Department's management system.

Alfred Marrow has now constructed for us from his participation in that effort and his wide experience in management, an extremely useful guide to modern government administration.

In recent years, new concepts of how best to get people to work together effectively have come from discoveries in the behavioral sciences, psychology, political science, and organization development.

These new approaches emphasize the need to humanize and to change the form of the traditional bureaucratic structure.

Such new management concepts, based on sound psychological principles, provide workable answers for the improvement of complex organizations. In industry, where they have been used with cost-effective commitment, they have been successful.

These new methods, I believe, can be made applicable to government agencies. What is more, they are not short-term, first-aid gimmicks. They are based upon hard-tested behavioral science facts collected by experienced business executives and trained psychologists.

The people who work in government can be turned either way, toward growth or toward stagnation. The design of the system in which they work can significantly influence which way they go—and how far. In government, the direction has been too often toward stagnation.

Our management leaders are just beginning to understand that their employees want to be trusted and consulted. People are now insisting on being allowed to participate actively in decisions relating to their jobs.

Whether the new management approaches are called democratization of work, participative management, or simply humanization of jobs, their objectives are the same: to improve the quality of life at work, and to thereby improve productively the quality of the work performed.

This book offers new ideas and tested ones that can provide solutions to urgent administrative problems. It provides many enlightening glimpses into the future.

It tells the story of a fascinating case study. At the same time, it offers a model that can be followed by governmental organizations. If adopted, these principles will help greatly to restore pride and self-esteem for employees of the American government, and effectiveness for its management leaders.

# Contents

# Chapter 1
## *The Need for New Major Changes*

*We trained hard, but it seemed every time we were beginning to form up into teams we would be reorganized. I was to learn later in life that we tend to meet any new situation by reorganizing; and a wonderful method it can be for creating the illusion of progress while producing confusion, inefficiency, and demoralization.*

—Petronius Arbiter
ca. 60 AD

Effecting change in the management system of any large, old-line organization is at best difficult. But when the particular target is the United States Department of State, often derisively called the "Fudge Factory," that task would appear to be nearly impossible. Yet, despite its long history and encrusted tradition, the Department has made positive progress in reforming its entangled and calcified bureaucracy.

This report describes how ideas for a new management system happened to arrive at the State Department, how they were planted, and who cultivated them. More remarkably, in the eyes of this writer—who was in the process from the beginning—it is a story that has succeeded despite many failures. It had its beginnings in 1964 and still survives in 1973, despite the harsh climate in which the ideas were planted nearly a decade ago.

The usefulness of a report like this is essentially to encourage the adoption of similar management principles in other organizations so that the ideas can spread and help the nation to win in the business of business and the business of government. Many mistakes were made and this report will point them out so that the reader will recognize them and understand how to avoid them.

How long the new concepts and practices initially introduced between 1964 and 1967 and renewed between 1969 and 1971 will survive, and whether or not they will flourish, is a matter of speculation. Morale in the Department had plunged with the shift in diplomatic power to Henry Kissinger and the White House. The fact that 6,000 people in the Department and the 6,000 abroad in American embassies were no longer involved with important issues of foreign policy created resentment among the professional staff. Now that Kissinger has been named to the top post there is hope that the decline in the Department's influence may end.

There is also new hope that a new deputy undersecretary of administration may be named. It is now occupied by an "acting" director because William B. Macomber, who was the deputy undersecretary for the past three years, has left his position to serve as ambassador to Turkey.

The writer can see indications that when a degree of normalcy returns, a management system stressing openness, trust, feedback, and broad participation in decision making will gain more popular acceptance among the vast majority of junior and senior members of the State Department staff and hopefully with the new secretary of state. The seeds sown from 1964 to 1967 were the seeds of a management revolution. In taking root within one of the biggest and most complex government bureaucracies, the ideas have proven in government, as they have in industry, irrepressible. The appointment of Henry Kissinger may signal a new lease on life for the Department. The secretary's seventh floor suite may become the energizer that the foreign service officers have dreamed about.

The State Department was established in September 1789, and is the oldest federal department. The secretary of state is the first ranking officer in the President's cabinet. As of the spring of 1973, the State Department employed 11,950 people, among them about 3,200 graduates of the Foreign Service Institute who have passed their foreign service examinations and are called foreign service officers.) These men (and a few, about 5 percent, women) mostly regard themselves as the State Department's elite corps and are proud and jealous of their rank, their perquisites, and the intellectual and social status implied by their FSO title. In a questionnaire, which will be explained more fully later, a representative group of FSOs was asked how they saw themselves; they replied: "Reflective, qualitative, humanistic, subjective, cultural, generalizers, men with intercultural sensitivity who are detached from personal conflicts in the performance of their jobs."

The State Department also has men and women who belong to the Federal Civil Service system. They are administrators, department managers, lawyers, secretaries, and so on; they do not go abroad with a commission from the President to execute the foreign policy of the United States as directed by the President. Persons serving abroad in these support-type positions are designated foreign service staff. There are also foreign service reserve officers who hold special five-year commissions to serve here and abroad. Most of these FSRs, as they are called, have joined the State Department because their work experience or training fulfills a special purpose.

For the past five decades the Department of State and its Foreign Service have been under criticism for failure to function efficiently. The Department has been examined, chided, experimented with, and reported upon again and again. Over the years critics have made the same charges of featherbedding, superfluous paperwork, and underemployment of human resources. The foreign service officers have been ridiculed in the press as "cookie-pushers in striped pants." The self-confidence of these officers has been shaken by years of acrimonious attack and frequent neglect. President Nixon has appointed as ambassadors to almost all the desirable countries in Europe people who were large contributors to his campaign. Lifelong career foreign officers have received their ambassadorial appointments to other capitals in the world, including such minor posts as Ouagadougou and Bujumbura.

To an extent that applied to State more than to most other federal agencies, the Department had earned the reputation of being an executive branch choked by red tape and restrained from acting quickly by an enormously long chain of command. It was administratively rigid and characterized by sluggishness, inefficiency, and overcautiousness. These faults could be attributed to its authoritarian organizational structure, its outmoded personnel practices, and its sanctified routines. Added to all this was the unavoidably intricate nature of the Department's relationships with Congress and the White House.

Many members of the State Department were aware that the department was overstaffed, especially by senior grade generalists. But a large number felt especially threatened by proposals for major changes made by outsiders. Though they recognized the imbalance between the available work and the oversupply of manpower, they did not see any of the recommended solutions as satisfactory.

The fact that Secretary of State Rusk was receiving 1,000 cablegrams every morning was offered by some defenders of the status quo as evidence of the immense amount of work that needed to be done. They did not agree with critics who claimed the voluminous reports contained nothing more than a bloated quantity of trivial and inconsequential information.

In 1962 the State Department was characterized by President John Kennedy as a "bowl of Jello." Bright, vigorous, slightly disrespectful young men in the Executive Branch were annoyed and irritated by the nineteenth century pace of State Department activity. They devised methods to bypass the State Department bureaucracy whenever speed in decision making was required. The long-pondered judgments of foreign service diplomats seemed far too timid for modern diplomacy and modern communications techniques. In the so-called crisis there was little time for on-the-one-hand, on-the-other-hand reasoning, or so it seemed at the time.

The State Department was simply not geared for quick, decisive thinking. It had grown and flourished in the days of Yankee Clippers and diplomatic messages sealed with red wax. At the time of World War II, the State Department had only 2,000 employees and was housed in a single building adjacent to the White House. Its diplomats were trained in the classic tradition, and proudly represented the United States overseas in the everyday business of relations between sovereign nations.

But when it came to the creative work of developing international policies for the President—be he Kennedy, Johnson, or later Nixon—the President chose quite pragmatically to rely on men he knew and trusted for their understanding of twentieth century politics and power. Only a few men in the State Department merited such presidential attention. Consequently, the State Department as an organization was generally belittled by the power structure in Washington, as is almost any organization that once was arrogantly strong and over the years grows defensively weaker.

# Chapter 2
## *From Theory X to Theory Y*

At a luncheon meeting with a small group of advisers, principally businessmen and behavioral scientists, one day in 1964, Secretary of State Dean Rusk talked about the Department's "core problem": getting people to accept and enlarge their responsibilities. Secretary Rusk knew when he said those words that in an organization where many bureaucratic practices had hardened, solutions to the problem would be extremely difficult. This writer, who was at that luncheon, can describe Secretary Rusk as skeptical that it could be done.

William J. Crockett, appointed deputy undersecretary of state for administration by President Kennedy in 1963, had arranged the luncheon and enlisted the support of Rusk. Crockett took on his duties following the inability of two capable administrators to reform the foreign service system. He recognized that a major reorganization was called for—one that would install and sustain an approach within the Department that encouraged among other major changes wider participation in problem solving and decision making. Only such a major change, he believed, would solve the problem of getting people to accept and enlarge their responsibilities.

State's management problems had already been surveyed by many experts and sweeping changes were always recommended. The report most often quoted within the Department—the Herter Study—made major proposals for changes encompassing organizational structure and methods of staffing and training the Foreign Service Corps.

A critic of the Herter Study held that "while it proposed changes that were relevant it would not receive the staff support to implement it." The foreign service officers feared another reorganization and were prepared to do everything they could to prevent it from occurring. Their resistance to the plan was not so much to its recommendations but arose from a realization that the organization changes would not be effective unless the interpersonal milieu were altered.

Chris Argyris, whose study will be described later, concurred in this belief. As he pointed out, the *"living system"* of the Department contained norms that inhibit "open confrontation of difficult issues and penalize people who take risks." The "living system" rewarded only certain types of interpersonal styles. It helps to create a perception of the Foreign Service as being a rather closed club; induces a degree of blindness on the part of the members concerning their impact on each other and "outsiders"; and generates an intricate network of organizational defenses that makes the members believe that changing it may be very difficult, if not impossible.

Crockett shared these misgivings. He knew that his management approach was considered unorthodox in many respects, and that his conduct in his previous position at the United States Embassy in Rome was used as evidence of this. "Results are more important than regulations," Crockett said. "Regulations are not chiseled in stone. They are printed on paper and, if it makes sense, they can be changed." Although his attitude created uneasiness among personnel who had lived by the book for years, Crockett persisted in creating innovative systems, setting goals, measuring results, taking risks, and making changes.

The spirit of the management approach that Crockett had introduced in the Rome embassy, he was now eager to implant in all the United States embassies. During his first year and a half in his new position in Washington, he had restlessly sought ways to implement a major reorganization. But as the chief administrative officer, an overload of routine matters demanded his concentrated attention elsewhere.

Crockett, at conferences with business leaders and in his reading of books on business subjects, had come across frequent references to the work of the late Douglas McGregor of the Massachusetts Institute of Technology—in particular McGregor's *The Human Side of Enterprise*.[1] He found the subject of the highest interest.

McGregor, he learned, focused on the conditions of management that would facilitate maximum growth in productivity. He conceptualized his ideas as Theories $X$ and $Y$ to contrast two opposed assumptions about human nature that underlie the authoritarian and participative systems of management. McGregor observed that conventional management policies were mostly Theory $X$, the authoritarian, which runs counter to what psychologists know about human nature.

McGregor believed that most people like work and will exercise self-direction and self-discipline to attain the goals to which they are committed. Under proper conditions they will not only accept but also seek responsibility. "The aver-

[1] New York: McGraw-Hill Book Company, 1960.

age person possesses a relatively high degree of creativity," McGregor stated, "and it is management's task to discover how to tap this reservoir to help solve mutual problems."

The traditional organization is guided by Theory $X$, to use McGregor's terminology. This assumes that man dislikes work, has little ambition, and prefers to avoid making decisions. Management's task in Theory $X$ is to supervise closely and to direct such people—to persuade, reward, punish, and lead them—in the classic carrot-and-stick approach.

Crockett recognized the classic Theory $X$ system in the State Department: hierarchical structure; emphasis on authority as the indispensable means of managerial control; detailed prescriptions for carrying out each job. He spoke optimistically of replacing the bureaucratic Theory $X$ model that typified the State Department's operations with the more flexible Theory $Y$ organization.

Through the suggestion of mutual friends, Crockett visited me in my office in New York. He spoke candidly of the Department's problems and the rough road ahead if he chose to reform the system. I suggested that the T-group training method (which I had described in a book called *Behind the Executive Mask*[2]) might be a helpful tool in bringing about a participative management system consistent with the Theory $Y$ philosophy.

During the next few months Crockett evolved a long-range plan and, in late 1964, felt ready to begin a number of substantial reforms. He realized that a large-scale action program of such scope would need substantial assistance from people of diverse talents and abilities from both outside and within the organization.

---

[2]Alfred J. Marrow, *Behind the Executive Mask* (New York: American Management Association, 1964). Revised edition in press under the title *The T-group Experience*, Publisher NTL Institute, Arlington, Va.

Here is what he did. He set up five separate groups of knowledgeable, experienced advisers to help him reform the practices in the Department and to give it a new administrative philosophy.

One group of advisers had three men of respected business and scientific credentials and distinguished backgrounds in large organizations. They would meet with Crockett at regular intervals for all-day sessions. These men were neither soft-minded nor faddists. They knew from personal experience the difficult problems of introducing a more participative system of management in large organizations. These men were E. Edgar Fogle, vice president of Union Carbide Corporation; Dr. Fred A. L. Holloway, president of Esso Research and Engineering Company; and myself, chairman of the board of the Harwood Manufacturing Corporation.

A second group consisted of teams of behavioral scientists who were recruited under a contract with the National Training Laboratories (currently the NTL Institute of Applied Behavioral Sciences) to lead one-week seminars using the T-group method of training. Here the participants would be placed in situations where they could take a clearer and more objective look at themselves and become more aware of their own behavior and that of the others involved with them.

A third group was composed of internal staff and outside experts who possessed specialized knowledge and skills. These included representatives from such diverse fields as art, architecture, building construction, food suppliers, education and others.

A fourth group was a scientific task force from the Institute for Social Research at the University of Michigan. Their assignment was to measure and evaluate the effectiveness of the program. They would observe all changes initiated, record how much was accomplished, and of what value. In sum, they would document the program and assay the results.

The fifth group was a consortium of outstanding behavioral scientists and individual State Department officers who were to develop and implement the program which was known as ACORD (an acronym for Action for Organizational Development). They were responsible for the broad administration of the program and served as the direct link with the training seminars led by the National Training Laboratories. They were also to act as a central base for developing and guiding the program, serving as a clearing house of communication and coordination and a source of support for line bureaus.

These five teams worked separately but all directed their efforts to help Crockett. The broad aim was to heighten the Department's effectiveness and to lead its people to find greater personal satisfaction in their jobs. Crockett's first important step in reducing layering came when Dwight Porter, assistant secretary for administration, went into the field to become an ambassador. Crockett gained the agreement of Secretary Rusk to abolish the level formerly represented by Porter, along with five other levels down to the basic operating units. These units were of various sizes and importance. But size was not Crockett's prime consideration.

# Chapter 3

## *Changing The "Living System"*

In June of 1965, Crockett announced what was called a major reform designed to reduce bureaucratic stratification. It was the formal word of the cutting out of six supervisory layers between Crockett and the operating managers. The announcement signaled the elimination of 125 positions and the transfer of 160 employees to other parts of the Department. Some of the operating units were to be broken up and some relatively powerful unit managers were about to be stripped of some of their former powers. The new program was to follow McGregor's Theory $Y$ managerial approach. Crockett expressed the hope that the reorganization would replace the spirit of authoritarianism in the Department. The announcement was couched in Theory $Y$ concepts—openness, participation, self-management, decentralized responsibility, management by objectives.

Interviews held at a later date with program managers by a research team from the University of Michigan found that the staff perceived the reorganization as an order. They were dismayed at the inconsistency of the preemptory way the reorganization was announced in contrast to the constant references to the new participative management concepts.

It is instructive for the record to see how Crockett outlined the rationale for his proposed changes. In July 1965, Crockett spoke to some 450 managers and employees of the administrative area (known as the "O" area). Here is the essence of his remarks:

> ... Our challenge is to find a structure—one which releases people from the obstacles and inhibitions of our highly centralized organization, thus permitting them to feel they are their own managers, with their own operations. Is there a way of organizing ourselves so that each of us can feel that we are a vital part of the whole?
>
> I believe that our present concept of decentralized management by objectives and programs will accomplish these objectives by: decentralizing our management into self-contained, semi-independent, and semi-autonomous programs, each with a manager; eliminating *every* intermediate supervisory level: delegating almost complete authority for daily operations to the program managers: ensuring that each program manager has the resources, the tools, the people, the money, the authority, the regulations, the means, and the conviction for attaining our mutually established goals.
>
> Of course, there are both objections as well as problems that we must face in getting this concept into being. What are some of the objections that have been raised?
>
> 1. Existing managers, within the hierarchial structure, will lose part of their operations. (Absolutely true. This is one of the reasons for the new plan.)
>
> 2. Many intermediate supervisory jobs will be abolished, and not all of these people like the idea. (Absolutely true. Again, this is one of the basic objectives of the plan.)
>
> 3. It is really not decentralization but super-centraliza-

tion, since all of the managers will report to the top man. (Not true. Each manager will be given almost autonomous operating authority with self-defined policies and mutually agreed-on objectives.)

4. The head man has too long a span of control; he can't supervise so many people. (Not so. Each manager will have his *own* program, and report only as he needs assistance. He will be freed from the usual concept of the old hierarchical control.)

Naturally, there will be some problems. The things that you and I must do together are the following:

1. We must define the general purposes and concept of your program.
2. We must state the general objectives and goals of the program as we see them. What do you think we can achieve next year? What will it take?
3. We must establish what kinds of authority you need to get the job done.
4. We must decide about whom you serve. Is your service really fulfilling their needs?
5. How can I be most helpful? How can you use me to accomplish your purposes and your goals?

Now what do I really expect of each of you managers? These are some of the main things: to achieve the goals we have set; to operate as if you were running your own business; to keep your operations, procedures, and regulatory materials up to date.

And now, what are the things that you can expect from me? This is a two-way street and you'll need assurances and help. The following things come to mind:

1. Full understanding and concurrence with the goals, and the resources and requirements for their attainment.
2. Availability in person or by phone when you need advice or counsel.

> 3. Support for the things we are agreed that you will need to attain your goals.

However persuasive seemed Crockett's brief for his changes, the old climate of suspicion, fear, and anger was only slightly improved. Grumbling, complaints, and fears were evident among those who had had no opportunity to participate in the decisions about the new system. The resistance these people created helped to limit Crockett's original objectives.

Interviews by the Michigan team with State Department officials about their reactions to having fewer layers of supervision showed they were generally pleased with the new system. For, instead of having to go through the division head, office director, deputy director of personnel, director of personnel, deputy assistant secretary for administration, and assistant secretary for administration, it was now possible to reach the deputy undersecretary directly in one step.

Under the traditional system, on any given issue, one or more persons in the six-linked chain of command would turn out to be overcautious, or additional staff members had to be approached for clearances. Before the reorganization, it could take as long as *six months* for an important problem or issue to reach the deputy undersecretary. Under the new setup, the program managers answered directly to the deputy undersecretary, with the director general of the Foreign Service acting as coordinator on occasion. The time lag had been cut to an average of *two days*.

Another significant change was in the policy of giving program managers greater autonomy in setting goals for their own units. Crockett wanted these men to become more involved and make more decisions in their day-to-day operations. This was effected by a plan called management by objectives and programs. As an initial step the program manager prepared a draft of his specific objectives, fixed the target dates, and estimated the resources needed to achieve them. This draft was presented to the deputy undersecretary. Once the projection was agreed upon and signed, it became the manager's operating charter for the fiscal year. Thenceforth, the manager was expected to carry out the day-to-day operations.

In a few instances the new procedure created anxiety for timid young officers who were suddenly deprived of the security of the traditional six-layered superstructure. The new process of saying to a lower-rank officer, "let's talk this over with Crockett," and thereby jumping six echelons of the hierarchy, led some lower-rank subordinates to try to impress the undersecretary by overstating their objectives while also underestimating their requirements.

Understandably, these initial reforms came in for criticism. Frequently, the objections voiced could be traced to the unsettling effects of major changes in a stronghold of tradition-laden bureaucracy, and to reactions of distress when familiar practices were drastically altered. But, in the main, much of the criticism was caused by a basic misunderstanding of what was going on. Much of the apprehension could have been alleviated if the people who feared the effect of the changes on their jobs had participated in the discussions about the changes and been given an opportunity to influence the final decisions.

This lack of staff involvement justifiably led to complaints. Staff members protested that their views were not asked for and declared much confusion would have been avoided if only they had been consulted.

# Chapter 4

# Building a
# Climate of Openness

Several months after Crockett's reform had begun, his three-man advisory group encouraged him to retain the services of a team of behavioral scientists to serve as change-agents and to use the T-group method of leadership training and executive development to help overcome the growing resistances to the internal changes. The National Training Laboratories (NTL), a nonprofit organization, was chosen to conduct a series of training seminars for staff in Washington and the missions overseas.

The NTL consultants expected that as a result of the experiential learning the participants would acquire new insights into the exercise of authority and the struggle for power, and that they would learn new ways to create an atmosphere in which conflicts could be resolved. They also would learn—possibly for the first time—how their own behavior was seen by others.

More than 200 foreign service officers, including a number of ambassadors and deputy chiefs of mission, attended these workshops during the next year. The training seminars were held away from the work site and usually lasted one week. An outside expert, a trained psychologist from the National Training Laboratories, served as group leader. An inside staff member handled the advance work, helping to identify issues, selecting participants, and organizing sessions.

During March, June, and August of 1965, three seminars were held at Airlie House near Washington, D.C. The leaders were Chris Argyris, then of Yale; Lee Bradford, director of NTL; and Warren Bennis, then of MIT. Each seminar was attended by twenty senior foreign service officers, divided into two groups of ten each. Most were of the highest senior rank, class II and class I.

Argyris and Bennis led the members of one group in a study of their behavior. They helped the participants to look objectively at their styles of leading people. They explored together how the operations of embassies, consulates, bureaus, and other divisional units might be improved. The experience was rated as "very valuable" by most participants. Some even described the seminar as one of the most meaningful learning experiences of their careers. Others were less enthusiastic, although later interviews indicated many of these participants were irritated at the manner in which they were "sent" to the seminar rather than at the workshop experience itself. Again, it was unfortunate that a number of the group members were coerced into attending.

Many of the participants in the group in which Argyris served as leader were deeply impressed by the outcome of their program. Argyris was asked if a summary of what happened at the workshops could be produced. The sessions had been taped, and Argyris promised a written report describing some of the major findings.

Argyris limited his observations to data from the tapes. He used for illustrations only those issues on which a majority of the group members were in agreement, and focused primarily upon the problems that were uncovered and not upon recommendations for correction. He was aware that by focusing on negative aspects he ran the risk that some might interpret his analysis as pessimistic and discouraging. He stated forcibly in a preface to his report that such was not his view. He was simply presenting a diagnosis of an organization that was outdated and somewhat closed. He said he was optimistic that steps could be taken to bring about effective change.

He also stressed that he was not blaming anybody in the Foreign Service Corps for the State Department's troubles. He said he was impressed by the competence, commitment, and critical objectivity of most FSOs with whom he had worked, and considered them to be a major source of strength of the Department. He stated unequivocally that his approach was directed at State as a "living system" and not at staff members individually.

To understand a major problem contributing to internal State Department conflicts, one must appreciate the accepted role of the FSOs as the elite of the Department. This traditional self-image of the foreign service officer as key man in the history of the diplomatic service has inspired antagonism. The hostility had become particularly bitter in recent years between the administrators and the FSOs. The FSOs felt deep resentment at the control wielded by administrators over budgets, assignments, and promotions. The administrators complained that they were treated as non-elite and were looked down upon as though their principal duty was serving as "car-pool" supervisors. These perceptions voiced of each other by both FSOs and administrators aggravated relationships.

These perceptions arose because prior to World War II FSOs were most often sons of prominent Eastern families who wanted to "serve mankind." After World War II, a selection method for new FSOs was established to test candidates, and this "test" was patterned after the traditional image. The results were selection of young men primarily from the Ivy League schools and Eastern establishment, generally the liberal arts scholar.

A revealing exercise was introduced by Argyris and Bennis at a T-group workshop conducted for top-ranking officers from both the Foreign Service and the administrative staff. Since unproductive divisiveness prevailed between the two groups the two leaders were eager to demonstrate how often communication was distorted by untested and unrealistic perceptions.

The participants were split into two groups: the administrators in one room and the FSOs in another. They were asked to discuss three questions and to develop a list of words or phrases that would summarize their answers.

The questions were:

1. What qualities best describe our group?
2. What qualities best describe the other group?
3. What qualities do we predict the other group would assign to us?

A brief summary of the results follows: The FSOs saw themselves as

*Qualitative*—They predicted the administrators would see them as *arrogant snobs*.

*Humanistic, subjective*—They predicted the administrators would see them as *cliquish*.

*Cultural, with broad interests*—They predicted the administrators would see them as *effete*.

*Generalizers, detached from personal conflicts*—They predicted the administrators would see them as *resistant to*

*change, inefficient, dysfunctional, vascillating* and *com-promising.*

On the other hand, the administrators saw themselves as

*Decisive, guts*—They predicted the FSOs would see them as *negative.*

*Resourceful, adaptive*—They predicted the FSOs would see them as *bureaucratic.*

*Pragmatic*—They predicted the FSOs would see them as *practical.*

*Service-oriented*—They predicted the FSOs would see them as *preoccupied with minutia.*

*Able to get along*—They predicted the FSOs would see them as *limited perspective, educated clerks.*

*Receptive to change*—They predicted the FSOs would see them as *defensive, inflexible.*

*Useful*—They predicted the FSOs would see them as *necessary evil.*

Now, in actuality, the foreign service officers saw the administrative officers as

- Doers and implementers
- Decisive and forceful
- Noncultural
- Limited goals
- Interested in form
- Jealous of us
- Drones but necessary evils

The administrative officers saw the FSOs as

- Resourceful and serious
- Respected
- Inclined to stability
- Dedicated to job
- Externally oriented

- Cautious and rational
- Masked, isolated, surrounded by mystique
- Manipulative and defensive

After the lists were drawn, the two groups met together. According to Bennis, they discussed the results in an intense, high-pitched, noisy, argumentative, and, after a time, thoughtful session. The similarities and marked differences in perception were made clearer. The new insight produced some lessening of antagonism and provoked some new thought that made the climate a bit less hostile to changes.

NTL, in its role as a provider of change-agents, reached a mutual decision with the ACORD group to train "internal change-agents." The NTL psychologists were well-schooled in participative methods, team-building techniques, strategies for conflict resolution, change-agent skills, and T-group leadership; and were properly preparing the ground for the future growth of Theory $Y$ ideas in the Department. State Department officers would receive basic instruction from NTL experts in the theory and practice of T-group training and team building.

The decision to train these State Department officers was among the most crucial and effective moves made in the initial states of management transition. The idea in this case was that, ultimately, the trained State Department specialists would replace the outside behavioral science experts in training other State Department people.

# Chapter 5

## *Evaluating the Program*

About fourteen months after Crockett's first reforms were ordered, I recommended that the time had come to measure scientifically what was happening to the attitudes and morale of the people in the State Department as a result of the changes. I suggested that Rensis Likert, director of The Institute for Social Research at the University of Michigan, be consulted about making periodic measurements to appraise the success of the efforts over a span of time. A team from the Institute, headed by Donald Warwick as study director, would do the job. They would measure, interpret, and analyze attitudes and behavior during this period of ongoing change.

The Michigan team began its study at once. The team anticipated that it would find the changes in the managerial system to have the most impact on the special program managers; then, in lesser order, on subordinate members of the staff. The research method employed to evaluate the effect was primarily personal interviews, questionnaires, and rating scales.

Illustrative of the types of questions and ratings used by the Michigan study team in evaluating the extent to which planned changes actually occurred, or in assessing the effects of them, are the following:

### Job Involvement

How involved do you feel in your job?

Intensely involved _____        Completely absorbed _____
Very little involved _____

### Job Enthusiasm

What are your feelings about your job?

Complete enthusiasm _____        Enjoy it intensely _____
Depressed or hostile _____

### Job Influence

How much influence do you have over decisions affecting resources for your program, either money, personnel, or other resources?

Very great influence _____        Modest influence _____
Almost no influence _____

### Job Influence

How much weight do you have in deciding the overall objectives of your own program?

Very great influence _____        Moderate influence _____
Almost no influence _____

### Managerial Autonomy

A. With how many people above you do you have to clear to get approval for a major change in the way you operate your program?

0—No one _____        9-10 Persons _____
More _____

B. How much scope does your job give you to take initiative in trying out new ideas about operating your program?

0—Complete _____        9—Very Little _____

To provide a basis for comparison, the respondents were asked on each question to rate the answers as of "now," "one year ago," and "two years ago." The questionnaire generally followed the following format:

### Decision Process

How much influence do you have over decisions for your program, either money, personnel or other resources?

| | Now | One Year Ago | Two Years Ago |
|---|---|---|---|
| Very great influence on resources | _____ | _____ | _____ |
| Considerable influence | _____ | _____ | _____ |
| Moderate influence | _____ | _____ | _____ |
| Limited influence | _____ | _____ | _____ |
| Almost no influence on resources | _____ | _____ | _____ |

For statistical analysis, each of the spaces on the vertical scales was assigned a numerical code ranging from 0 to 9. The Michigan team summarized their preliminary findings as follows: The stripping away of six layers of hierarchy had increased managerial autonomy. Typical responses from those interviewed were:

> Before, there was horrendous layering. I reported through so many people that it was hard to get action to do anything. The first year was a revelation. I had direct access to Crockett. It was excellent.

> It has cut down on clearances and red tape. You've got to be sure that what you do is correct, but it is less frustrating when you see things being accomplished.

Those most directly touched by the structural reorganization—the managers in the personnel and in the management planning units—enjoyed the greatest increase in autonomy; those furthest away—the managers in the budget and the compliance and operations areas—gained the least.

Despite these favorable results, some negative comments were elicited. Several of those interviewed spoke of feeling isolated by Crockett's decentralization moves. They experienced frustration because, if a good job were done, no one was near enough to notice it. This troubled Crockett. It raised the question of the readiness of some managers to stand on their own feet. If they were highly dependent, needing to lean on superiors for support and continuous approval, the new program threatened them. Crockett recognized that there was no simple answer other than a better method of early identification of men with independent leadership qualities. But this was unrealistic under the Department's outdated system of selecting men for promotion.

Another problem brought up in the interviews was that of inadequate or erratic resources, especially in the allotment of funds to develop the new program. Crockett conceded the validity of such complaints but commented, "The fact is that we have to wait for a budget to be approved. This year [1966] we didn't get an appropriation until late September. This means that our appropriation takes longer to get distributed. It's a difficult thing. Too bad, but we are grown-up people and ought to understand."

The reform program was also designed to increase the program managers' role in the decision-making process. Here, the evaluation of results was also positive in these key areas:

1. On decisions affecting program resources the survey noted a moderate increase of influence exercised in the special program unit along with a slight increase in the personnel, budget and compliance, and management planning units.

2. In matters that affected the operation of the programs, subordinates were found to be in possession of a net increase of influence on their superior's decisions.

3. On power to formulate program methods there was an average increase for the entire group, with personnel recording the greatest increase and the other units following with slight improvements.

To appraise the extent to which communication was affected by the reorganization the research team used four measures of efficiency: frankness between unit managers and their superiors, with other "O" area units, with units outside "O," and with subordinates in each manager's own group.

The study reported moderate to slight gains in communication in all four areas. The greatest improvement in access was between managers and their superiors and with other programs in the "O" area. Smaller advances were noted elsewhere. Communication with units outside "O" and with subordinates in the individual manager's own unit showed modest increase for all program managers.

The new system had a negative impact on a few managers who complained of longer delays in communication despite the advantages of the reduced layering. Investigation revealed that this complaint was well-grounded. In the preceding six months Crockett had been away on trips for about five months. His absence revealed a weakness in the system. Crockett was responsible for advance preparations for several overseas trips by President Lyndon Johnson. He accompanied the President on those trips. His time available for department consultation was further reduced because of his attendance at personal meetings with congressional members and White House staff.

The program was supposed to heighten incentives for better performance within the operating units. Here, the Michigan evaluation research team concentrated on obtaining ratings on specific aspects of job performance such as the clarity of the unit's objectives. the manager's skills and abilities, and the accomplishment of the unit's tasks. The findings generally supported the Crockett objectives.

The measurements of the University of Michigan team showed that the net effect of the changes on the motivation and attitudes of the program managers was positive, with managers reporting a greater sense of involvement and enthusiasm, but with varying differences among the units.

A number of unexpected difficulties were discovered. The most serious was a reduction in coordination. The Crockett reforms resulted in excessive fragmentation. There was uncertainty about responsibilities, little direction from above.

The appointment of five group coordinators was supposed to prevent some of these difficulties. Instead, it merely added more problems. This occurred because the 39 unit managers never fully understood the role and duties of the new coordinators. Despite these negative aspects only four of the 39 program managers indicated that they wished to return to the pre-1965 organization pattern. Most of the comments that came out of the interviews were in the nature of suggestions for improving the newer system.

Now before reporting further on the effects of the changes, it is important to describe briefly some areas of special resistance:

The first of three very stubborn resistance points, and the easiest to identify, was the historic antagonism in the functional (economic, political, and so on) and regional or geographic (European, Latin American and so on) bureaus toward any attempt by the administrative area to impose change on them, or on the Foreign Service. Second was the resentment of a number of groups to having been excluded from participation in the planning of the reforms. Third, confusion resulting from the changes because other organizational changes were also in various stages of completion.

In general, however, the regional bureau response reflected positive attitudes toward the new system. The delegation of authority gave its staff greater flexibility and freed them from the burden of securing certain clearances from "O." As a result of the fewer bottlenecks and reduced paperwork, functional bureau officials also reported a number of advantages. Among them were greater savings of time, increased ability to respond to the needs of the embassies, and improvements in the bureau's handling of its own affairs, especially greater control over resources.

One of the least successful of the second series of changes in 1966 was the creation of an executive group to assist Crockett in managing the administrative area. The formation of this executive group was in response to persuasion from his superiors—Secretary Dean Rusk and Undersecretary George Ball—and from pressure from his own staff. Although Secretary Rusk and Undersecretary Ball had encouraged Crockett to proceed with the first stage of his reorganization in 1965, they grew concerned that he might be moving too fast and too far. For example, they believed his span of control was excessive. As Crockett put it:

> The executive group was introduced to establish the "window dressing" for the "span of control" problem because this was a persistent problem on the part of my bosses. . . . There was often a question of "How can you supervise so many people? Isn't the span of control limited to about seven, eight or nine people? How can you 'control' thirty or forty programs?" . . . the word "control" was very much in evidence and I was trying to explain that there wasn't much need for super-

vision. . . . But the Secretary expressed concern. He asked, "What do you substitute for the hierarchy? How do you ensure that it isn't running off in all directions without much guidance?"

Thus the weight of authority from above was to have a hierarchy within a hierarchy. But the pressure from my own staff was equally insistent. They wanted greater clarification of the functions and responsibilities of the special assistants whom I had appointed as coordinators.

The problems of coordination were not limited to budgetary issues. Both coordinators and program managers insisted that a group should be formed with the power to make decisions and to deal with the self-serving interests that followed the one-to-one relationships between myself and the program managers.

Thus, responding to the pressures from above and below Crockett set up the executive group. Unfortunately, not all of the members were as loyal to Crockett's efforts as they would have him believe. Crockett described its purposes as follows:

My concept was that almost anything that came to my desk was something that the executive group might take on. I was willing to relinquish much—most all of the authority—so that I wouldn't be a single authoritarian voice in it. I was willing to play the game absolutely open in dealing with the executive group.

You give up all your downward responsibilities. You take on some upward responsibilities. You take on the responsibilities that come to this desk because—if you don't there's double layering.

Now the question is whether they believe this totality— whether they, as individuals, are willing to play selfless parts in this.

Crockett evidently considered the members of the executive group as a "council of elders," staff members with no line responsibilities. In actual practice, however, the members of the executive group found it difficult to separate themselves from their roles as line managers. Moreover, the original memorandum establishing the executive committee did not specify the duties and functions of the group. The ambiguity was a mistake that created misunderstandings and interfered with the smooth functioning of the group throughout the fleeting seven months of its existence.

It is fair to say that the executive group accomplished little. A contributory reason for this failure may have been a recurrent rumor on the grapevine to the effect that Crockett was planning to resign. The members of the executive group interpreted the spreading gossip as a signal to move cautiously. Understandably, they hesitated to make any changes that could jeopardize their position under a new undersecretary. As soon as rumors of his departure traveled through the grapevine the thrust of the reforms was almost immediately blocked. Some of the change-resistors breathed a sigh of relief, anticipating that the Department would return to its previous measured pace and comfortable routine. Others hoped that Crockett's successor would continue the spirit of innovation. But they, too, took a position of caution, holding back on all action. The gossip soon proved true.

Crockett's impending resignation was not wholly connected to the reorganization program but the strife caused by reforms did play a large part. Crockett had been aware that changing the practices and managerial philosophy of a long-established traditional institution is extremely difficult and drawn out.. He had expected to meet resistance but not as strong as it turned out to be. But the attacks on "Crockett's Rockettes" were growing more frequent and more intense.

His superiors in the Department were not supportive. Congressmen were demanding more of his time for hearings. President Johnson was planning still more trips abroad and Crockett was expected to deal with the intricate details of these trips and to accompany the President. Budget problems plagued him. The job stresses seemed to be growing too great. Some FSOs were giving overt lip service to the reforms but were covertly sabotaging some of the programs. The progress of reform was sluggish. He feared that there could be a negative presidential reaction if distorted reports of shattered morale were leaked to the press. When the job offer from IBM was made, Crockett accepted it. Simultaneous with the announcement of his resignation, he left. It was in January 1967, about 18 months after he had started the reorganization program.

Although Crockett's efforts had resulted in a number of significant changes, he knew that many were not working well. Some had been too hurriedly planned and others too impulsively improvised. In addition, it was directed too largely from the top and, of course, there was too little participation in the program by the staff.

Crockett's program, many felt, had made sense in many ways. Continued progress seemed inevitable. Crockett, himself, in personal conversation with me expressed confidence that the momentum would continue. But as was soon seen, he was mistaken. Changes of a very different sort were in the winds.

# Chapter 6
## *Sudden Death*

Idar Rimestad, whose experience was limited to his having worked in a traditional hierarchial structure, replaced Crockett. His immediate previous position had been as administrative counsel at the Paris Embassy. Crockett was consulted in the selection of his successor and from all available information he approved of the appointment.

As an old-line administrator Rimestad had little interest "in making waves." The rumor soon spread that the Crockett program, especially the newer and more controversial aspects, would be eliminated or drastically altered.

Before long Rimestad made it clear that he considered the new system a mess. Reading some of the preliminary reports of the Michigan research team, he reacted with anger. It was ridiculous, he declared, in one of our infrequent conversations, to spend money on a project that found so much that was negative to report. He contended that negative information simply encouraged an expression of dissatisfaction by every employee answering the questionnaire or being interviewed. When Rimestad learned that the procedure recommended by the Michigan team is to feed back the collected data to the staff and then involve them in seeking solutions, he responded by suggesting that the University of Michigan cancel its contract.

Donald Warwick of the University of Michigan explained to Rimestad that all the data had already been collected and was being processed for a final report. The information had already been fed into the computer and was being analyzed and interpreted. After some hard bargaining Rimestad cut $25,000 from the contract. The remaining sum was adequate to complete the analysis of the data. To complete the study and publish the results, Professor Likert received a grant from a private foundation.

Rimestad also cancelled State's contract with the National Training Laboratories. Shortly afterward, he told his staff that he saw no value in continuing to use specialists from industry and the professions, even though they had been volunteering their time and talent. Rimestad initially showed his uneasiness at the presence of eminent business executives and outstanding behavioral scientists and responded by using his power to have them removed. He now aimed to return State, as quickly as possible, to its former bureaucratic format. The ACORD program was liquidated at the end of 1967. Line supervisors were restored to their old jobs.

In the spring of 1967, after about four months in the new post, Rimestad appeared at a congressional appropriations hearing. The appearance occurred a short time after the publication of Chris Argyris' report on "Some Causes of Organizational Ineffectiveness within the Department of State." The report had become a best seller in government agencies in Washington. Widely discussed, it created strong feelings pro and con and brought an avalanche of letters—some heated, many admiring—to the editor of the American Foreign Service Association's official magazine, *The Foreign Service Journal*.

Congressman John Rooney, chairman of the House Subcommittee on Appropriations for the various departments, including state, heard about the Argyris report and obtained a copy. In a budget hearing Rooney expressed his displeasure at the report. He was irritated because he was uninformed about the project until the interest created by the report was brought to his attention by congressional colleagues.

Rooney questioned Rimestad at some length. The following is a partial transcript of the hearing:

*Mr. Rooney:*    Are you familiar with this document entitled, "Some Causes of Organizational Ineffectiveness within the Department of State" by Chris Argyris?

*Mr. Rimestad:*  Yes, sir; I have read the report.

*Mr. Rooney:*    How much did it cost to print that?

*Mr. Rimestad:*  Approximately $1,500.

*Mr. Rooney:*    Who is this fellow Argyris?

*Mr. Rimestad:*  He is a professor at Yale University.

*Mr. Rooney:*    Has he ever worked for the State Department?

*Mr. Rimestad:*  To my knowledge, no. I should correct that. He had a contract to write this particular document; but aside from that he has not been on the rolls.

*Mr. Rooney:*    How much did he get for writing this?

*Mr. Rimestad:*  $3,000.

*Mr. Rooney:*    What do you think of this? I may be being unfair to you in asking this question at this time in view of the short period that has transpired since you took over the post of deputy undersecretary for administration, and if you feel that way, let me know.

*Mr. Rimestad:*  No, I am quite willing to comment on it. I have no exception to a study. I do not agree with this study in its rather clinical approach; it's a very small sampling of people. I think we could have arrived at this type of information without spending $3,000. I also do not agree with having it printed for the public distribution. I think it should have been for the use of officials of the Department and the Foreign Service. . . .

It should be noted that Crockett regularly briefed Chairman Rooney and members of the House Appropriations Subcommittee on matters that might be reviewed at budget hearings. Further, this line of questioning between Chairman Rooney and Crockett would have been vigorously defended and clearly explained by Crockett, who was fully familiar with the entire background of the Argyris report.

This episode seemed to stiffen Rimestad's resolve to go back to Theory $X$ authoritarian bureaucracy.

The Argyris report was not meant to create a furor.[3] Argyris wanted it to serve as a summary for the participants of what could be learned from the T-group experience. Second, it would support the movement for change from within the State Department. He reasoned that sending the report to the participants could create a dialogue among senior foreign service members who had been exposed to the reforms. Such a dialogue might add constructively to processes for change fermenting within the State Department. Argyris had initially sent complimentary copies only to the participants in the group who had met with him. But the interest in the report was widespread.

For example, one senior foreign service officer, who had not been involved (and therefore had not received the document), told Argyris that the report seemed to be suppressed and was more difficult to obtain than one officially stamped top secret. He cautioned Argyris that persons such as Senator Fulbright might learn of the document and accuse State of suppressing surveys critical of the Department. Indeed, when the report was published, Senator Fulbright's office called Argyris to ask if it had been censored in any way. Argyris replied that no censorship had been attempted. The implication of censorship concerned not only Argyris but other key foreign service officials who

[3]Letters that appeared in the *Foreign Service Journal*, June 1967, appear in the Appendix.

wanted to bring about internally instituted change within the Department. Several top-level foreign service officers met to discuss this. They decided that even though Argyris had no interest in distributing the report, keeping it confidential could lead to trouble and be of limited use. Critics of State might accuse the Department of suppressing controversy, an accusation very wide of reality. To prevent that possibility and to symbolize the Department's genuine interest in diagnoses and improvement, it was agreed that State itself ought to publish the document. Crockett, as deputy undersecretary, volunteered to write the introduction; and the Government Printing Office published the study.

Despite the constructive aims of Argyris, Crockett, and the foreign service officers who had urged that the analysis be made public, the reaction of some others, including a few members of the Washington Press Corps, was negative. Some interpreted the report as a blistering attack on the State Department and the Foreign Service. Ill feelings were expressed at the survey being made public, a reaction expressed even by some FSOs who fully agreed with its accuracy.

Arguments over making the report freely accessible were heated and acrimonious. In the highly charged emotional atmosphere many critics overlooked the simple fact that Argyris had first cleared the printing with Crockett and that the deputy undersecretary had, himself, written the preface.

In his preface Crockett gave the following detailed explanation of his reasons for having the report published:

> The Department of State has been fortunate to have had Dr. Chris Argyris of Yale step out of the academic ranks, even if briefly, to devote his wide background in the behavioral sciences and in administrative practices to serve us as a kind of alter ego. And I mean an alter ego in the finest sense of that phrase; as a friend and confidant.

The efforts in organizational development, and the examination of the Foreign Service which engaged Chris Argyris' attention, stem from an exploratory kind of seminar held at Airlie House in midsummer of 1964. At that meeting some twenty senior foreign service officers began to explore some of the means by which they, as individuals using ideas developed in the social and behavioral sciences, could relate to their work, their co-workers, and their organization in new and significant ways.

Since then, several hundred officers of the Department of State have taken part in such training experiences. I have done so myself, and I think, along with me, that most of these officers would subscribe to the thesis that, though one may have little doubt concerning one's professional capability when each day's crises arise, it is only slightly short of a revelation to search out and perhaps to discover our true personal location within the web of organizational relationships we have—the very concerns which have so engrossed the author of this paper for so long.

The decision to publish a study of this kind, or to publish it without censoring the quotations, was not taken lightly. Large organizations in general are not noted for being candid about internal problems and differing viewpoints. We also recognized the fact that the sessions in which this material was developed were problem-oriented. This naturally produced a strong bias in favor of what was wrong. Consequently many of the good things about the system, including its strengths and the deep dedication of its people, or the prevalence of positive attitudes about the organization, are not reflected in the paper. It would have been much easier not to publish Dr. Argyris' work for fear that the material might be twisted out of context or otherwise treated unsympathetically.

Several considerations argued against such a cautious attitude. The first was the realization that, if we really are breaking new ground in our organizational development program, it would behoove us to take this risk—to be open about the ambivalent attitudes, feelings, and frustrations of the people who constitute the "living system."

A second realization was that the quotations appearing in this work, with minor changes of time and place, could have been uttered by persons in any large organization; that what we are dealing with here are problems typical of all large enterprises (private and public) and not alone of the Department of State. This, indeed, is a point that Dr. Argyris himself stresses.

Finally, the most positive reason is that being honest and open about the problems dealt with in this study offers the best beginning for dealing with them effectively and constructively.

These are one skilled observer's views of a highly complex, diversified organization; an expert observer's partial sample. They are presented in the hope that they will be tested against the Department's collective experience to stimulate a continuing examination which will improve this essential institution through which we all serve the American people.

We shall need the understanding and support of all its members if we are to achieve the goals we mutually seek.

The Argyris report presented an objective and unvarnished summary of the actual taped statements made by FSOs during their week-long T-group seminars. The FSOs spoke rather candidly of the norms that are created and maintained by the members of their organization. These norms act as guidelines that influence the behavior of everyone in the group.

The majority of the officers and career officers in the seminars described norms of the following kinds:

*A tendency to withdraw from interpersonal difficulties and conflict.* This withdrawal eventually included stifling dissent as well as avoidance of tackling substantive issues that might, if discussed forthrightly, lead to conflict or personal embarrassment. This caused all types of bureaucratic maneuverings in order to reach other people "indirectly," "carefully," "safely."

*Not being open about interpersonal problems or substantive issues that could be threatening to others, especially superiors and peers.* Over long periods of time this made it difficult for people to know how much faith to place in what others were saying. Consider these remarks:

*Officer A:*   I think that one reason I have succeeded is that I have learned *not* to be open; *not* to be candid.

*Officer B:*   I have experienced situations where I sensed the superior was not leveling. I figured that he was trying to predispose me to his point of view.

*Officer A:*   And what did you say?

*Officer B:*   Not a darn thing.

*Distrust of aggressive or openly competitive behavior in others.* For example, if someone became angry the strategy was to hold back feelings. As this way of reacting grew evident the FSOs reported that they soon learned to mistrust their own and others' politeness. After all if their own politeness was a facade then probably this was true of the others.

As one might expect a norm also existed that the appropriate response to aggression was to *withdraw and to judge the other man negatively, but not to tell him.* In other words, to avoid active confrontation. For example.

*Officer A:*   I tell you, there's nothing more upsetting than suddenly realizing that the guys I have badgered have no response—just silence.

*Officer B:*   So for you, silence hurts.

*Officer A:*   It hurts deep.

Argyris reported how FSOs feared being engulfed by "the

system." He recorded their hopelessness about ever changing it. For example, FSOs condemned "layering," yet admittedly continued to rely on it and, in some instances, expand it. They questioned the selection and promotion processes, yet when asked to provide viable alternatives were unable to do so. As a consequence of frequent withdrawal and lack of self-confidence they were burdened with guilt.

Argyris perceived a powerful circular loop, a process within the Foreign Service's "living system" that prompted the participants to ward off interpersonal threat by minimizing risk taking, not being forthright, as well as reducing feelings of responsibility, and evading open conflict. This, in turn, reinforced those who had already decided to withdraw, play it safe—"not to make waves"—and to do so both in their behavior and writing.

Under these conditions, FSOs soon learned the survival quotient of "checking with everyone," developing policies that upset no one, taking positions in such a way that their superiors had to bear the responsibility for them. This attitude encouraged layering; more people were needed to make a decision, and protection of one's "bureaucratic skin" was the prime concern. This meant that most departments were overstaffed; there was "safety in numbers," if a crisis arose.

Argyris also held a separate series of thirty-one interviews. with younger FSOs some six months prior to the foregoing analysis. The questions he asked of the younger FSOs were not derived from his later analysis of the older ones. Not all the issues brought up during the subsequent training seminars were discussed at interviews with the younger FSOs, but there was high agreement among them about what were their critical problems. The views they held did not contradict those expressed by the senior officers.

The young FSOs confirmed that the Foreign Service community was characterized by (1) suppression of interpersonal issues, (2) minimal openness and trust, (3) withdrawal from interpersonal difficulties and conflict, (4) little risk taking and acceptance of responsibility, (5) overdependence on the superior, (6) crisis orientation, (7) cautious memo writing, and (8) an attitude of "don't make waves."

Excerpts from several letters published in the *Foreign Service Journal,* June 1967, may provide the reader with a sense of the positive feelings the writers expressed toward their one-week T-group training experience.

> I'm prepared to testify personally that the value of my week of T-group training *was higher than of any week of Foreign Service Institute training to which I have been exposed.*

> The discussion brought underlying tensions into the open where they could be looked at and discussed in a way that clearly had not been possible within the office itself.

> The necessary atmosphere could only have been generated and the issued posed so helpfully with professional help from outside the office.

> One key question—and doubtless not a unique question—dominated the talk. Why couldn't the system be more open? Why did so many FSOs play their cards so close to the chest?

> In my judgment there has been a significant improvement in "teamwork" in the office since the session.

> The voluminous work done for the military by the social scientists seem to be of little interest at State. This is so even though the new ideas, insights, and techniques (of the behavioral scientists) might well simplify and make more exact large parts of our work.

A number of critical letters were also received. These focused primarily on the decision to publish the findings.

# Chapter 7

## *A New Life*

In October 1969, Idar Rimestad was appointed to a special ambassadorial post in Geneva, Switzerland. The transfer of Rimestad was routine. He was eager to shift to the less turbulent atmosphere of a traditional embassy and had bid for the post when it opened. William B. Macomber replaced him. Macomber had previously served efficiently as assistant secretary for congressional relations and as ambassador to Jordan. His appointment was greeted favorably both within the Department and outside.

There was no doubt that the new President, Richard M. Nixon, was dissatisfied with the operations of the State Department. During his presidential campaign in October 1968, in a speech delivered at Dallas, he said, "I want a Secretary of State who will join me in cleaning house in the State Department. It has never been done." It was with the departure of Rimestad and the arrival of Macomber that the management ideas seeded five years before with Crockett began to show new signs of life.

The new leadership of the State Department—Secretary William Rogers, Undersecretary Elliot Richardson, and Deputy Undersecretary William Macomber—was faced with strong pressure from the White House in 1969 to develop a reorganization program. The President said that he wanted the Department's managerial capacity strengthened through the use of modern techniques.

About the same time pressure also came from the American Foreign Service Association (AFSA), a professional organization of foreign service officers. The drive took the form of an AFSA report published in the summer of 1968 that reflected the discontent of junior officers which had first manifested itself in late 1966.

During the same period, the Junior Foreign Officers Club asked serious questions about the character and direction of the Department as a whole. In mid-1967 a group of young FSOs, in an election, took over control of the American Foreign Service Association on a platform that called for "some zeal." They wanted more professionalism, more influence on decisions of major importance in the areas of administration and personnel, and a new vision of the future of the foreign affairs community.

In early 1973 the AFSA, by employee balloting, was selected to be the exclusive bargaining organization to represent the interest of all foreign service personnel in its relations with management. In effect, the AFSA became an independent professional union.

At the urging of a group of FSOs, and in response to the President's order to make the State Department more effective, Elliot Richardson invited Professor Harry Levinson of Harvard University, and this writer, to meet with him, William B. Macomber, and several top members of their staff. The plan agreed upon was for an all-day, uninterrupted conference on the goals of the previous reorganization attempts.

At the meeting Richardson asked me why the previous

effort had failed, why the goals were still unmet, and if I believed a wholly new organization development program in State could succeed and how this could be accomplished.

Both Levinson and I responded affirmatively, but with some skepticism. We emphasized the need to build trust and openness into the "living system" of the Department, and to establish a problem-solving atmosphere where creativity rather than conformity would prevail. We pointed to the existing "living system" in which the norm encouraged minimum risk taking, evasion of open conflict, and avoidance of personal responsibility. We deplored the enormous waste of talent that resulted from excessive layering and needless controls. Finally, we cautioned Richardson and his staff not to repeat the failures of the past by bringing in outside experts. If they wanted to risk another reorganization they should have the Department undertake to change itself from within. A massive self-study might bring some reform. Our advice was that action by external consultants alone would surely fail.

My own experience with numerous organizational studies by professional experts had made me aware of the shortcomings of this approach. Few people trust the experts' work. Employees feel threatened. Eventually the report is received, heatedly discussed, and then quietly filed and forgotten. It rarely leads to lasting reform. It is this problem—to get a dynamic nexus between fact-finding and action—that led Levinson and myself to urge a self-study. It was probably the only answer to the question, "How can facts be found in such a way that the findings will lead to effective change?"

I stated that it has been my experience that a self-study can be carried out with a high degree of technical competence. Since a self-study is performed by the internal staff the facts they uncover are their own and are taken seriously.

The likelihood is much greater that this will lead them to press for action because of their personal involvement. The features that emerge form a self-survey are not a caricature by some "busybody" from the outside. Traditional practices have been observed and their features drawn by several hundred colleagues. The final picture may not be flattering but it is a true likeness without anything faked or hidden. Too many people "are in the know" so a coverup is not possible. But precisely for this reason the original can, and will, be improved.

Richardson and Macomber, of course, had other choices open to them. They could employ an outside firm of consultants, they could appoint a panel of leading citizens, or they could use a variety of other methods. After further discussion among themselves and with Secretary of State William Rogers, Richardson and Macomber agreed that the Levinson-Marrow recommendation of self-study conducted by an in-house set of task forces would be most likely to tackle the problem successfully. The widest possible participation by all FSOs was to be encouraged.

*Now, you may sense, the seeds were growing.*

On January 14, 1970, Macomber spoke at a large meeting of executives in the West Auditorium in the Department of State headquarters building. His chief theme was that a reform program, particularly of the management strategies currently practiced in the Department, was imperative and that Secretary Rogers and Undersecretary Richardson attached great importance to such a project.

He added that all members of the Foreign Service knew that there were many outside the Department who would happily impose their ideas on how to reform the organization. There had been rumors some time earlier that Senator Fulbright was planning a full-scale hearing on the effective-

ness of the Department. But Macomber pointed out that the
secretary and undersecretary believed that outside efforts
would not be as effective, nor as informed, as those em-
barked on by the staff members themselves. Some outsiders
claimed that the job could not be done from within.
Macomber said he did not agree with them.

Macomber then spoke of the helpful studies that had
previously been made by his predecessors and how useful
this preparatory work would be. He mentioned he was
certain many of the recommendations that would be made
would be extracted from those earlier impressive efforts. He
affirmed his confidence in the staff and stated that in his
view the competence level of the foreign service officers
was unexcelled.

He then added, in his comprehensive 3,100 word speech,
that

> ... from a management point of view, our critics have
> more to go on. ... To use a modern phrase, *management
> has not been our bag.* ... We are an organization which
> has traditionally been comfortable with policy-making. ...
> But we have tended to be *intuitive in nature, weak in
> planning, and unenthusiastic about management.* In retro-
> spect, it is clear that these change-resistant instincts have
> caused a great share of our difficulties. ... The key fact is
> ... either we produce the improvements necessary to
> meet this challenge or, as I have suggested, this will be
> done for us. ...

> The diversity of personnel and function ... *dramatically
> underscores* the premium we must place on the develop-
> ment of coordinating and management skills. ... An abso-
> lutely essential requirement for our future ambassadors,
> deputy chiefs of mission, assistant secretaries, deputy
> assistant secretaries and counterparts in our sister agen-
> cies is the capacity to manage.

He warned that if the organization did not come up with the recommendations for improvement that "it will be done for us." He then stated that the program would start immediately. Task forces would be set up to review and recommend improvement in all the operational areas.

The response from the staff was enthusiastic. Soon thereafter thirteen in-house task forces, working under the title "Diplomacy of the 70s," were organized. Their aim was to study basic questions that troubled the State Department: recruitment, building a personnel system, employee attitudes, performance appraisal, openness of communication, early identification of executive potential, establishing goals, training in management and executive skills, encouraging constructive dissent, and others.

So that these kinds of questions could be examined and discussed in a very frank spirit, Macomber set rather loose guidelines. The task forces were to operate as they, themselves, saw fit, and then freely offer their recommendations.

The thirteen task forces comprised more than 250 career professionals of State, and forty officers from other foreign affairs units, such as the Agency for International Development and the United States Information Agency.

Macomber's speech inspired a new spirit within the Department. There was a resurrection of many parts of Crockett's earlier plan. The task forces chairmen were chosen from the most outstanding men in the Department. Four were ambassadors; five, deputy assistant secretaries; and four, office directors. The assignments to the committees tended to center around these objectives: "How could the State Department improve its management capability, insure the full and favorable utilization of its abundance of talented personnel, and make itself a more creative and open institution?"

The members were selected through a nomination system and through volunteers. Macomber and his staff carefully avoided suggesting chairmen or task force members. The policy was clearly stated that this reform program was to be the work of the Foreign Service. Each task force was composed of about twenty members.

Each group set its own meeting schedules. They were given complete freedom to examine any problems in their assigned area and come up with whatever recommendations they chose. On the average the task forces met weekly— sometimes at luncheon meetings and often in the evenings. The time spent on the project was in addition to the members' regular duties.

The issues stimulated heated debate. Through interviews, questionnaires, examinations of earlier studies, and open meetings, facts were collected and recommendations formulated. Earnest discussions were held with key executives and then with staff at all levels of management. Draft reports were circulated to the embassies abroad.

By the end of November, slightly less than a year later, a summary report was written by Chris Petrow, an able member of Macomber's staff, and presented to the secretary of state. In addition each task force submitted its own report as well. The 13 reports, when combined, totaled more than 600 pages and contained an astonishing number of recommendations—slightly over 500. The process was probably without precedent in the history of any government agency.

Secretary of State William Rogers had been briefed during the preparation of the summaries and quickly approved about 400 changes in principle. A few of the remaining recommendations needed further study and some were rejected.

Macomber was directed to begin the implementation of

the approved recommendations at once. On July 6, 1971 he could report that about 75 percent had been put into effect.

The self-study demonstrated that it is possible for members of an organization to take a critical and objective look at themselves. People who know most about their problems are likely to be more comprehending in their findings and more foresighted in their recommendations than are outside experts. The self-study also proved that almost everyone who participated found it to be a tremendous learning experience. Many misconceptions were cleared away while the staff officers examined how things were done and how and why inefficiencies occurred.

Finally, all who participated recognized the need for a continuous process of self-renewal and self-examination, in an atmosphere in which all were free to express themselves with the utmost possible independence and originality.

At a talk given to departmental personnel in February 1972, Macomber reviewed what had been accomplished. He described the self-study as

> ... the most comprehensive and searching critique ever written about the Department ... no other document can match it.... The diplomat's job is more important and more complicated than it ever was.... We need a broader range of skills and expertise; and because of the participation of so many other elements of our government in foreign affairs, our diplomats must now be managers, coordinators, and leaders to a degree undreamed of by their predecessors of a simpler age....
>
> The past two years have been a time of turmoil. There have been criticism, disagreement, and public controversy.... We are in a much better era now.... No effort of this kind starts without antecedents. Much of the credit must go to those career officers among you who, in

increasing numbers in the years immediately preceding January 1970, pressed for reform and set the stage for what has followed. To you, and to the many who joined you in the past two years, we owe a considerable debt.

For the first time, under the reform program, members of the Foreign Service will have an important and formal voice in the development of all personnel policies—policies which play such an important part in their lives and careers. . . . Furthermore [he added] modernization and reform, if they are to be really effective, require the development of an increasingly effective, fair, and enlightened system of human relations. . . .

Here, too, we have had a remarkable two years with much progress being made. . . . What has emerged is a system under which the men and women of the Foreign Service can have a real voice in the policies and regulations affecting their careers.

Such self-study had enabled the officers of the Foreign Service to find out where they stood and where they were not going to stand. They had become emotionally involved. Their roles were that of participants rather than mere observers. Their shared experiences prepared them psychologically to accept the implications of their findings and freely to accept changes in values, attitudes, and practices.

Secretary of State Rogers said about the report

The efforts we are making in-house speak very well for the vitality and dynamism of the Department and the Foreign Service. I continue to believe that if we could leave behind us an improved and modernized system for dealing with this country's foreign policy problems, this could well be a more lasting and significant contribution to the public interest than success in handling many of the more transitory matters which necessarily occupy our attention.

Petrow, Stern, and Levinson[4] pointed out that bureaucratic organizations cannot be changed from the top because downward control is limited by tradition, policy, and other constraints. They cannot be changed from within because no one person has the authority to change the work of the others. They cannot be changed from the outside because the inside staff will resent the intervention by people outside the system.

Therefore, successful changes in any system are likely to occur only when there is simultaneous pressure from all three sources: the top, the inside, and the outside. This rare combination of forces occurred in the fall of 1969 when President Nixon called for reform. Pressure was being exerted from the inside by the American Foreign Service Association, from the outside by Congress and the public, and from the top by Secretary Rogers and President Nixon.

[4]C. Petrow, T. Stern, and H. Levinson, *Management Review* (December 1971).

# Chapter 8

## The Future

What of the future? How long will the new order last? Will it be wholeheartedly implemented? There are many difficult questions. Do organizational changes, successfully introduced over a relatively short span of time, survive permanently? Does an organization so altered continue the new direction and pace of change? Does it become stabilized or does it gradually revert to its earlier condition? We are not yet equipped with the answers. These are some of the reasons:

A good part of what will happen depends on the impact the new recommendations will make on the "living system" of the Department and on those harmful practices that were described in the Argyris report: withdrawal from interpersonal difficulties, distrust of others, judging another person negatively but not telling him, avoiding other forms of confrontation, playing it safe—"not making waves."

Of equal importance will be the answer to the question— will some of the enthusiasm that produced the constructive recommendations continue during the painful shift from a predominantly "authoritative" to a dominantly "participative" system? After so many major changes some retrogres-

71

sion is certain to occur. How much reinforcement will the new system require to survive?

There are other uncertainties. Many of the maladies that affect the internal system are still there: the traditional rivalries within the Department, the eight separate personnel systems, the feeling of elitism cherished by the FSOs, the question of whether the key executives really possess a coherent management philosophy.

From the positive point of view there are a number of constructive forces working toward stimulating a new kind of "living system." The self-study unlocked a store of energy; a rich resource of ideas has been made available.[5]

The authoritarian system is on the decline. A participative order is rising. This is true in all organizations. [Even in the FBI Clarence M. Kelley, the new director, has endorsed the idea of "participatory management"—a concept inconceivable in the regime of J. Edgar Hoover.]

William Crockett, former Undersecretary of State for Administration, read the manuscript of this volume in the spring of 1973. In his comments on the organization development program he stated:

> I agree with the general conclusions in your book about some of the reasons that we didn't produce better results. But I believe there are other learnings too, that will plague any organization that endeavors to change.

---

[5] As evidence of the changing climate we quote from a statement by Undersecretary for Political Affairs William J. Porter before members of the 107th Class of Foreign Service Officers at a swearing-in ceremony held on June 15, 1973. "Modern diplomacy requires new skills, and one of these is management. We have come a long way in recent years to take ourselves in hand, to apply our skinny resources where and how they will do the most good. And we have come to include in our judgment of an individual his skill as a manager. Look upon yourselves as managers, first of all, of yourselves and of your day."

In the political environment of government, no one has much "time" at his disposal to carry on a series of change programs. Certainly it was my feeling (belief) that time was my most implacable enemy. And while I agree we really did try to do too much too quickly, temptation will inevitably face any administrator who has a limited tenure.

The most serious mistake I made, I believe, was to try to inject the programs as a top-down reform, using tough Theory $X$ methods, and by relying too much on the diagnoses of outside experts, task forces, study groups, advisory bodies, and so on. I'm sure their diagnoses were accurate and their prescriptions for changes correct, but the patient didn't even admit to his illness, so the diagnoses were strongly denied and the medicine, when administered, was bitter and punishing.

Macomber's method of using internal task forces for the diagnostic process was much better and had a much better chance of being accepted by the entire group. Self-criticism and diagnosis are often exciting, positive processes, but one can only be defensive when too many outside experts tell us what is wrong with us.

Another error I made was that I had insufficient insight into the way my new organizational concepts of autonomy and ownership may have threatened the individual who had neither the experience nor the psychological basis for such drastic exposure to freedom. We did not have a "people development" program that would have helped frightened and uptight individuals make such a transition. For, in the end, no organizational scheme will work unless the people involved make it work. The same thing happened when President Kennedy abolished the OCB and expected the State Department to fill that vacuum. Few did.

But in looking back, I have few regrets. I would make the same effort but, hopefully, with a better involvement of people at all levels. However I am convinced that the traditional hierarchical system of management (little changed since the days of Moses) does not fulfill man's basic needs for dignity, freedom, and individual self-worth. It is authoritarian and antidemocratic.

Precious little R&D is going on in American organizations today for finding different (better) ways of linking people together in the work situation than the way we now do it in most of our institutions. I believe the widespread alienation, apathy, and credibility gap that exist between all segments of people and the establishment, come, to some extent, from our failure to make work a more exciting and fulfilling experience for all of us. To the degree that my State Department organizational experiment provided a little early R&D on an alternative way, and a more exciting way for many, of linking people to their jobs, then to that degree the effort was worth the cost to me personally—and the vision it gave to some that there were (are) better ways.

Obviously the implementation of the changes Crockett refers to will have its costs. And these will have to be paid for in coins of time, authority, and prerogative. But for the State Department the rewards will be renewed pride, heightened performance, and growing strength.

The pressure for reform continues to be strong. The uncertainty at the top has been resolved. Henry A. Kissinger, who has asserted that he abhors bureaucracy, has been named secretary of state. As a person of intellectual capacity and experience it is expected that he will recognize the craving of the department staff for a greater participatory role.

It is possible that there will now be simultaneous pressure from all three sources—the top, the inside, and the outside. If so, successful changes are likely to occur and remain. For when people at work have once experienced a taste of openness, trust, and the climate of participative management, they develop the strength and the strategies to cling to it.

# Epilogue

## *The Success of Failure*

By WARREN G. BENNIS, Ph.D.

Sometime around mid-March of 1965 I received a cablegram from Alfred J. Marrow asking if it were possible for me to participate in an organization development program planned by the Department of State. At the time I was professor of Management and Organizational Psychology at MIT's Sloan School of Management, on temporary duty in Calcutta heading up a small group of MIT professors attempting to establish one of two new schools of management in India. I was attracted by the clear significance of the State Department project, and the opportunity it offered to test some applications of behavioral science research. I was intensely interested, and so I arranged to take a one-month leave from Calcutta and return to the United States for the month of May 1965.

A good portion of May 1965 was spent in a variety of "OD" activities for the "best and the brightest" of State's top echelons. Following that, I engaged in intermittent counseling there over the period October 1965 (when I returned to MIT) through 1967.

Then the program was abruptly stopped, the various contracts terminated, and the in-house members of State (ACORD) shuffled off to sundry sanitary and safe activities either in State or other departments of government. All this was coupled with Bill Crockett's resignation. I felt certain that "OD" was conquered by organizational sludge, that the "best and the brightest" would sink and suffocate slowly, quietly, and imperceptibly—like those early dinosaurs who kept marching into the mud, sinking up to their eyes and recognizing, too late, the end of their species. Sinking and drowning in fudge may be sweeter, but death comes no less certainly at an early age.

Now, as a result of Marrow's remarkably honest and straightforward near-autopsy of this program—and what a welcome relief it is compared to the usual pap and apologies accompanying unsuccessful "social programs"—we learn that "OD" is still alive and recuperating in Foggy Bottom. This is thanks to Richardson's resuscitation, Marrow's persistence, Crockett's guts, and Argyris' blunt instruments of truth. We also see—and this is most important—that the lessons learned by the men and women were not forgotten by them. The values of "OD" once initiated, accepted, and adopted by people could not be so easily suppressed nor turned off—at least not permanently—anymore than human nature could be. And most of all, "OD" is simply a program whereby the basic elements of human nature can be expressed directly and openly.[6]

Many things are to be learned from this detailed report, so many that it should be required reading for all agents of

[6]Warren G. Bennis, *Organization Development: A Primer* (Reading, Mass.: Addison-Wesley, 1969).

change in our society, whether they be behavioral scientists, consultants, management practitioners, or whoever.

- We learn, for example, that change is a slow and painful process, and that patience (let alone skill) is a rare commodity among understandably important and frustrated executives.

- We learn that successful change cannot be accomplished without the coordination of three major elements working at essentially the same rhythm and speed: the top, the rest of the organization, and external forces (for example, Congress, the media, salient institutions affected by the change). Revolution from the top, Crockett style, no matter how just and right, no matter how true and beautiful, can cause more problems than it is established to cure.

- We learn that for any change program to be effective, those people affected by the change must be involved to some extent in developing it (how much remains to be seen), that they must trust in the initiators of change, and that the goals of change must be reasonably clear and explicit to all those concerned.

- We learn that any significant change will create significant enemies. There is no easy option here, except courage, persistence, energy, openness to error without fearing to embrace error, competence, and again Biblical patience.

- We learn that the agents of change must work with the healthy parts of the organization and not react too strongly to the "side elements." The sick will not be easily cosmeticated.

- And we learn that any program which attempts to reveal the basic humanity of all peoples regardless of how our institutions tend to create "pseudo-species" through specialization, competition, and interorganizational rivalry cannot be suppressed. Truth will win out. Inevitably. Painfully. Willfully.

It would be a mistake to read Marrow's report as either an indictment of the State Department or of the behavioral scientists who participated in the program or as an esoteric study of an exotic organization. The State Department is no more an endangered species than most institutions where 90 percent of our employed population now work. *All* organizations experience a similar lack of candor and openness, a like "pluralistic ignorance" (where everybody believes that everyone else *believes* something and then gives lip service to it, even though they really don't believe what everyone else seems to believe.) The Emperor's New Clothes fallacy is more than a good children's story. It is a story for grownups whose innocence is imperiled by traditions, norms, beliefs, values—mysteriously communicated, more mysteriously accepted and internalized—all of which makes them *say* they see beautiful clothes woven from gold thread when what they really see is a vulnerable old man in the buff.

I am writing this epilogue two days after the long testimony of John Dean III before the Ervin subcommittee inquiry into the Watergate affair. If one needs further evidence of the need for "Organization Development" at State, one need look no further than Dean's testimony *regardless* of whether or not his description of executive behavior leads to criminal or civil indictments. What we do know for sure is that the "best and the brightest" can be transformed by the tyranny of blind forces that somehow or another insinuate their way into people's minds and hearts in all the institutions in which we live and work.

"OD" is simply a way that attempts to open up and understand these forces better, to see whether or not such institutional norms (however expressed—through a wink, a glance, a cold shoulder, a removal from an invitation list, a rebuke, and the like) facilitate or disable our collective aspirations.

I salute Dr. Marrow and others who have had the courage to explore their own perspectives and norms. They have made it possible to restore confidence in ourselves and others who will not be misled, who can finally snatch success from failure—though it may be by the skin of our teeth.

*Warren G. Bennis, Ph.D.*
*President*
University of Cincinnati
July 1, 1973

# Appendix
## *Letters to the Editor*

# The Argyris Technique

I would like to add my comment to those that have cautioned against a too hasty rejection of the conclusions of the Argyris report. Those of us who have not actually participated in one of the study groups must of course withhold a final opinion on the overall value of the operation. However, we may still ask that the powers that be give the possibilities of this technique the most serious consideration.

I think we should be especially careful to do so because of our institutional predilections. In the past 20 years, the Department and the Foreign Service have shown relatively little (although increasing) hospitality to the findings and techniques of the social sciences and the humanities, although the work being done in these fields should be, as a matter of course, part of our regular stock in trade. In fact it seems that the voluminous work being done for the military by the social scientists— which ought to concern us and interest us as much as a new wrench should intrigue a plumber—seem to be of little interest here. This is so, even though the new ideas, insights, and techniques especially of the last ten years, might well simplify and make more exact large parts of our work. (Not everything the social scientists have to say assays out as pure gold; the lesser ones produce a spectacular amount of trivia, usually written in Choctaw.)

Nor have we shown any special talent for institutional adaptability in the face of demands for change from outside our institutional borders, or those called for by historical change. The price of institutional freedom is usually the willingness to seek out the need for, and administer internally the self-regenerating steps required by changing times and changing circumstances. If this simple (and universal) rule of institutional survival is not heeded, a price is exacted and it is usually the loss of more rather than less freedom of action. The history books and political science texts are full of examples, and no group of people is more directly concerned professionally with them or should know them better than the Foreign Service. I think it can fairly be said that the unhappy price for our institutional failure to read the signs accurately, and adapt to Congressional demands for some lateral entry in the early 1950s, and thus head off Wristonization, is now being paid for by its victims.

Stewart Alsop wrote an eloquent piece in a recent *Saturday Evening Post*, enjoining the world (including Mr. Argyris) to leave the Foreign Service and the Department alone. I agree. I also believe that the way to insure being left alone by our critics is to so manage our own affairs that no reasonable grounds for outside tinkering exist. Perhaps the Argyris technique is one way to develop the continuing critical, institutional self-examination I believe we need. Perhaps it is not. But since our forte does not especially lie in adaptability or willingness to innovate, we should be particularly careful to compensate, in fact over-compensate, for these sometimes fatal bureaucratic deficiencies. We must force ourselves to consider carefully what is new, whether we want it to appear on our doorstep or not.

*William M. Kerrigan*
Washington

## Record of an Experiment

Chris Argyris, in my judgment, is neither entirely right nor entirely wrong. Argyris, in focusing on the interpersonal problem, has put his finger on a part of the problem. He fails, however, to recognize that the alleged inefficiency of the State Department is more a function of the complexity of the world in which we live than of either organizational or interpersonal inadequacies. The most significant fact about foreign policy remains that any government's influence in dealing with foreigners, or even its own citizens, is limited. Yet we certainly do need to improve our performance, and clearly, we should try to learn what we can from the social psychologists.

Now it is commonplace to note that the principal asset of the State Department is its personnel. If exposure to the social psychologists leads to a significantly better performance by only one or two officers (to say nothing of the several hundred participants so far), it is not inconceivable that the overall savings to the

US will far exceed the costs. If we accept three propositions:

— first, that the Foreign Service has something to learn:
— second, that the professional social psychologists have something of value to impart; and
— third, that how FSOs handle or mishandle situations can have momentous consequences.

the odds make social psychology at several hundred thousand dollars a year a good betting proposition for the State Department. I'm prepared to testify personally that I believe the marginal utility to me—and I hope to the Department—of the expenditure on my week of "Sensitivity Training" was higher than that of any week of FSI training to which I've been exposed. Of course, language and other training in skills is indispensable but it takes longer and costs more.

I would like to report on what John Stutesman called "a mini-lab" involving myself and my immediate colleagues in the Office of Atlantic Political-Economic Affairs (EUR: RPE). It was my experience that the officers of RPE and I benefited from a "team-building session." It concentrated on the process of office operation, rather than on operating issues. RFE's experience, though a limited one, may be of some interest.

Following preliminary discussions with the staff, it was eventually decided on a collective basis to give social psychology a try, despite a great deal of skepticism.

Accordingly, the entire staff met outside the office one Friday from noon until almost midnight. It would not be right to say that anything sensational developed. Far from it. And it is probably true that there were few surprises for any of the participants. Nor, obviously, was there time for "head-shrinking." Yet, the discussion brought a few underlying tensions into the open where they could be looked at and discussed in a way that clearly had not been possible within the office itself. Nor, and this is an important point, could the necessary atmosphere have been generated and the issues posed so helpfully without professional help from outside the office. Among other things, officers could and did light into the Office Director apparently with less concern over the consequences than in the normal office setting. The Director and the other participants enjoyed this; especially the other participants.

One key question — and doubtless not a unique question—dominated the talk. Why couldn't the system be more open? Why did so many FSOs play their cards so close to the chest? Virtually everyone wanted to know more about what was going on at higher levels in the Department. Over and over, the question was asked, "What the hell goes on here, anyway?"

At the same time, general staff meetings were criticized for being boring, for their failure to focus on significant issues and for their inflexibile routine. The limited office staff meeting in which the Director, Deputy Director and the Officers-in-Charge participate appeared to intrigue non-participants. There was a demand to receive guidance more directly from the top. The discussion permitted others to point out that pressures of time and requirements of efficiency often made this impossible.

The group discussion was also of some interest in focusing on roles in the Department. I was surprised to

discover that there was a good deal of simple misunderstanding about this, coupled with a sense of remoteness from senior officers. Yet the patent inability of principals in a large organization to deal regularly with all of the staff was recognized as beyond remedy. Still, airing a shared frustration by itself seems to have helped make it less of a cause for officer discontent.

Some minor bureaucratic feuds between RPE sections and officers were brought into the open and freely discussed. These were incipient troublespots about which I was well aware and which I was trying to control. The group examination of the relations broadened my understanding of what the different officers concerned thought was at stake. More important, they developed a different perspective on the RPE effort as a whole and a new insight into colleagues' aims and motivations. In my judgment, there has been a significant improvement in "teamwork" in the office since the session.

A critic may reply that neither the meeting nor explanations should have been necessary. I can only testify that they were. And I believe morale has improved as a result, with all that that means in performance terms.

There were other concerns that emerged as well. There were tensions and resentments caused by problems with secretaries, by pressures to put in overtime, and by difficulties in transportation. They are now at least better understood, even if we are still struggling with remedies.

The discussions also revealed frustration at the lack of comprehension elsewhere in the Department and in other parts of the RFE operation. A number of officers thought it would be well to extend team-building sessions to include representatives from other parts of the Government with which RPE frequently finds itself in conflict. There is much to be said for this. Adversary proceedings—too frequently conducted as bureaucratic battles—have their value. But could they not be conducted with more of an eye on the cooperative purpose?

All of the points set down here now seem obvious. There was probably a certain prior awareness of all of them. Perhaps with more sensitive leadership changes, including variations on the staff meeting theme, would have been made without the team-building session. But one of the values of the team-building technique and of the ACORD Program generally is that it forces participants to think systematically and analytically about issues which are all too often relegated to the background or even deliberately suppressed.

*Deane R. Hinton*
Washington

### Reductio

Your article about the "Argyris" report, the report itself, and correspondence about it in the *Journal* lead me to conclude that foolish questions elicit foolish answers.

*Jo W. Saxe*
Washington

*Editor's Note:*
*The correspondence on this subject is now closed.*

# Biography

*Alfred J. Marrow, Ph.D.*

Alfred J. Marrow holds a Ph.D. in psychology and has for many years been an outstanding figure in the fields of group dynamics and organization behavior. A Diplomate of the American Board of Professional Psychology, he now serves as its president.

In the course of an eminent and interesting career he has held the posts of Commissioner of Human Rights of the City of New York, chairman of the board of a major manufacturing corporation, trustee of Antioch College, The New School for Social Research, Gonzaga University, and the National Training Laboratories.

His life work has been devoted to building bridges between the behavioral sciences and the management of people to attain a more harmonious social order. In a practical pursuit of that goal he has developed the theses expounded in this volume.

He is the author of ten books, translated into eight languages. Reviews and readers have joined to praise his pioneering contributions. He has written the scenarios of two popular educational films and played a leading role in both. Currently, he is writing and producing a two-hour film on the T-group experience for developing human relations skills.

His professional honors include listing in American Men of Science; a citation from the New York Academy of Science for Scientific Achievement; laureate of the Kurt Lewin Award—the highest honor in the field of social psychology; and the U.S. State Department citation for distinguished service.

He currently serves as psychological consultant to organizations in higher education, government, and industry.

93